Introduction

Knitting looms are the fast and fun new way to knit. Now you can learn new stitches and knit up a variety of items for yourself, your family and your friends. The designs in this book will introduce you to creative stitch patterns, and utilize a variety of yarns. Loomers of every skill level will find something new and exciting to knit.

Keep warm with the Bordered Scarf and matching Woven-top Hat, or the fun-to-knit and fun-to wear Popcorn Bobble Hat. Dress up any outfit with the Mobius Shawl or Diamond Lace Shawl. The Seed Stitch Spa Set and Drawstring Purse are quick-to-knit projects that make great gifts.

Knit the Chevron Baby Blanket to welcome a child, or the Shell Stitch Afghan to decorate your home. Pick up your loom, some yarn and this book, and *Learn New Stitches on Circle Looms* today!

Design Directory

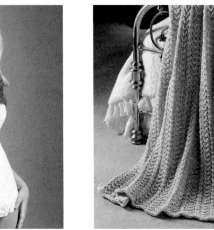

Stitch Directory

Garter Stitch
.................................page 10

Loom Weaving
.... page 12

Popcorn Bobble Stitch
.................................page 14

Eyelet Stitch .... page 16
I-Cord...................... page 16

Seed Stitch
.... page 18

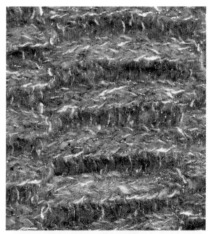

Checkerboard Stitch
.... page 20

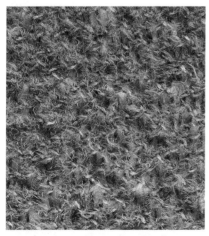

Diamond Lace Stitch
.... page 22

Shell Stitch
.... page 24

Chevron Stitch
.... page 27

Materials

Knifty Knitter™ circle looms from Provo Craft. (Photographed items were designed with the Knifty Knitter circle looms. Although you can use other knitting looms, such as the In the Attic Looms, the peg count and gauge may be off.)
Hook tool
Crochet hook
Small split ring stitch markers
Tapestry needle
Scissors
Measuring tape

Techniques
Casting On

Crochet Method

1. Make a slip knot about 6 inches from the end of the yarn.

2. Insert the crochet hook into the loop of the knot.

3. Catch the working yarn with the crochet hook and pull a new loop through the slip knot.

4. Put the slip knot loop onto peg 1 of the loom and put the new loop onto peg 2 of the loom.

5. Insert the crochet hook into the loop between pegs 2 and 3 on the loom, and holding the working yarn to the inside of the loom, catch the working yarn with the crochet hook and pull a new loop through.

6. Put the new loop onto peg 3 of the loom.

7. Continue creating new loops and putting them on the pegs until the desired number of pegs have loops on them.

E-wrap Method

1. Make a slip knot about 6 inches from the end of the yarn. Place it on peg 1.

2. Starting from the inside of the loom, bring the working yarn between pegs 2 and 3 to the outside of the loom. Continue wrapping peg 2, bringing the working yarn between pegs 2 and 1 to the inside of the loom.

3. The yarn will cross over itself on the inside of peg 2 as it travels to peg 3.

4. Continue wrapping the pegs until the desired number of pegs have loops on them.

Basic Stitches
Stockinette Stitch
Stockinette stitch is the knit pattern created by knitting every row.

E-wrap (Twisted Stockinette) Stitch
Multiple pegs can be wrapped before knitting them off.
1. Cast on with the desired method. This puts one loop on each peg.

2. Start with the yarn on the inside of the loom.

3. Wrap the peg counter-clockwise with the yarn ending up on the inside of the loom.

4. Continue to the next peg. The yarn will cross over itself on the inside of the loom.

5. To knit off, insert the hook into the bottom loop on the peg. Lift it over the top loop and off the peg to the inside of the loom.

Flat (Stockinette) Stitch
This stitch is the equivalent of the knit stitch made with knitting needles.
1. Cast on with the desired method.

2. Bring the working yarn in front of the peg, above the existing loop.

3. With the hook tool, lift the bottom loop over the working yarn and off the peg to the inside of the loom.

4. With the hook tool, pull on the new loop making it looser by bringing in a bit of the working yarn.

Note: *This stitch needs to be loose or your knitting will become very tight; and it will become nearly impossible to knit off the pegs after several rows. The flat knit stitch should use the same amount of yarn as the e-wrap stitch.*

Garter Stitch
Garter stitch is the knit pattern created by knitting one row, then purling the next.

Purl Stitch

This stitch is the opposite of the flat (stockinette) stitch. It is the equivalent of the purl stitch made with knitting needles.

1. Cast on with the desired method.

2. Bring the working yarn in front of the peg, below the existing loop.

3. Insert the hook tool into the existing loop from the top. Place the hook over the working yarn.

4. Twist the hook tool into the peg to catch the working yarn, bringing it through the existing loop.

5. Pull the hook tool away from the loom, creating a new loop with the working yarn.

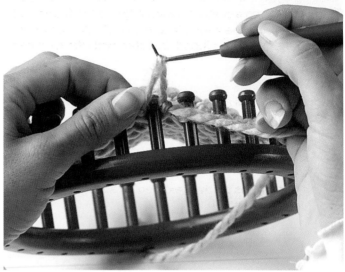

6. Remove the existing loop from the peg and move it to the inside of the loom.

7. Place the new loop on the peg.

8. Pull on the working yarn to tighten up the new loop a bit if necessary.

Additional Stitches

Slip Stitch

The slip stitch can be used at either edge of a flat piece. This stitch gives a pretty braided edge to the fabric, but does not add to the width. To slip a stitch, do not wrap the peg that is to be slipped, but start with the next peg.

Eyelet Stitch

This stitch creates a small hole in the fabric which can be useful for drawstrings or buttonholes.

1. Knit to the place where you want an eyelet. Move the existing loop on the peg to the next peg.

2. Bring your working yarn in front of the empty peg.

3. Knit both loops on the next peg as a single loop when wrapping and knitting it off.

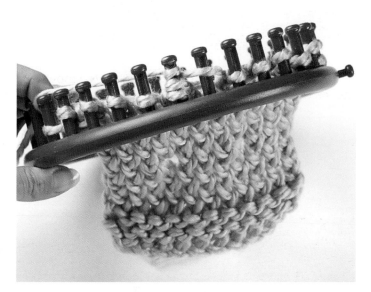

4. On the next row, treat the working yarn in front of the empty peg as a loop and knit it as usual in the pattern.

Checkerboard Stitch

See directions in Mobius Shawl pattern on page 20.

Ribbing Stitch

See directions in Drawstring Purse pattern on page 16.

Seed Stitch

See directions in Seed Stitch Spa Set pattern on page 18.

Popcorn Bobble Stitch

See directions in Popcorn Bobble Hat pattern on page 14.

Chevron Stitch

See directions in Chevron Baby Blanket pattern on page 27.

Diamond Lace Stitch

See directions in Diamond Lace Shawl pattern on page 22.

Shell Stitch

See directions in Shell Stitch Afghan pattern on page 24.

I-cord

1. Make a slip knot and put the loop onto peg 1.

2. Bring the working yarn from the inside of the loom around peg 2 to the outside of the loom.

3. Bring the yarn between pegs 2 and 1 to the inside of the loom.

4. Bring the yarn around peg 1 to the outside of the loom.

5. Bring the yarn between pegs 1 and 2 to the inside of the loom.

6. Bring the yarn around peg 2 to the outside of the loom. There are now two loops on each of the two pegs.

7. Knit off pegs 1 and 2.

8. Repeat steps 3–7 until the I-cord is about ⅔ the finished length. (It will stretch.)

9. With one loop on each peg, remove the loop from peg 2 and put it on peg 1.

10. Knit off peg 1.

11. Wrap peg 1 and knit off.

12. Cut the working yarn, leaving a 6-inch tail.

13. Wrap peg 1 and knit off. Insert the hook tool into the loop on peg 1 and pull on it until the end of the yarn comes through the loop. Pull snug against the I-cord.

14. Thread the yarn tail onto a tapestry needle and run the needle inside the I-cord for several inches to hide it.

Starting a new length of yarn in the round or in the middle of a row

A new skein of yarn can be started at any point in the row. This technique generally works better with thicker yarns that won't show through to the right side of the fabric.

1. Complete the last stitch with the first strand of yarn.

2. On the next peg, make a stitch with the new strand of yarn to secure the yarn, leaving a tail several inches long.

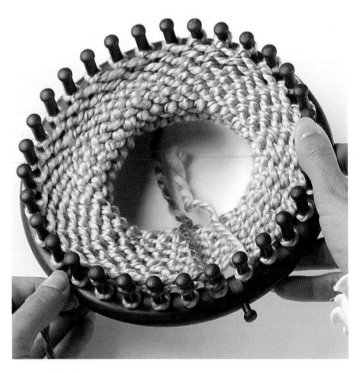

3. Continue wrapping and knitting in pattern.

4. After several rows have been knit, a hole can be seen in the knitting where the new yarn was started. Twist the two yarn tails together once, filling in the gap, with each end doubling back on itself.

5. Weave in ends.

Starting a new length of yarn on the edge of a flat piece

When knitting flat pieces, it is easy to switch yarns at the end of a row. This is the recommended method when using thinner yarns where tails woven in the middle of the piece might show.

1. Complete knitting a row.

2. Wrap the new yarn once around the last peg knit.

3. Knit off this peg by bringing the bottom loop over the two top loops.

4. In the next row, bring the two bottom loops over the top loop.

5. When you finish the piece, weave in ends.

Binding Off
Flat bind off

When knitting the last row of the piece, make sure the loops on the pegs are loose enough to easily reach the adjacent pegs. This prevents your bound off edge from being too tight.

1. Start at the end opposite from where the working yarn is.

2. Move the loop on the second-to-last peg onto the last peg. If this is a difficult stretch, the loops on the pegs aren't loose enough. Make the last loop you knit very large, pulling from the working yarn, so it is about 3" in diameter. Adjust all the loops in order, distributing the slack to each peg along the loom. Repeat if necessary.

3. Knit off the last peg.

4. Move the remaining loop to the vacated peg.

5. Continue moving the second-to-last loop to the last peg and knitting it off until there is one loop left on one peg.

6. Wrap the peg and knit off.

7. Cut the working yarn, leaving a 6-inch tail.

8. Wrap the peg and knit off again.

9. With the hook tool, pull on the loop on the peg until the cut end of the yarn comes through.

10. Gently pull snug against the knit fabric.

Gathered bind off

1. Cut the working yarn, leaving a 6-inch tail.

2. Cut a length of yarn about 3 times the distance of the pegs being used, and thread it onto a tapestry needle.

3. Run the tapestry needle through each loop.

4. If your piece is circular, run the needle through the first loop again.

5. With the hook tool, remove the loops from the pegs.

6. Turn the knit piece inside out and gently pull on the two ends of the length of yarn to gather the knit fabric.

7. Tie the ends securely, including the yarn tail, when tying the knot. Trim and weave in ends. ■

Bordered Scarf

A garter stitch border makes a nice edge along this easy scarf.

Skill Level

EASY

Sizes

Youth, adult
Instructions are given for smaller size, with larger size in parentheses. When only one number is given, it applies to both sizes.

Finished Measurements

Youth: 3½ x 50 inches
Adult: 7 x 65 inches

Materials

- Lion Brand Wool-Ease Thick and Quick super bulky weight yarn (6 oz/106 yd/170g per skein): 1 (2) skein(s) grass #131
- Green Knifty Knitter round loom (36 pegs)
- Hook tool
- Tapestry needle
- Crochet hook

SUPER BULKY (6)

Gauge

4 inches = 9 stitches, 12 rows
Gauge does not need to be exact.

Pattern Note

All knit stitches are twisted (e-wrap) stitches.

Instructions

Crochet cast on 10 (20) pegs.

Row 1: Slip peg 10 (20), knit to end of row.

Row 2: Slip peg 1, P8 (18), K1.

Row 3: Rep row 1.

Row 4: Rep row 2.

Row 5: Slip peg 10 (20), knit peg 9 (19–18), purl peg 8 (17–16), knit pegs 7–4 (15–6), purl peg 3 (5–4), knit pegs 2–1 (3–1).

Row 6: Slip peg 1, knit peg 2 (2–3), purl peg 3 (4–5), knit pegs 4–7 (6–15), purl peg 8 (16–17), knit pegs 9–10 (18–20).

Rep rows 5–6 until scarf reaches 49 (64) inches.

Rep rows 1–4.

Bind off using the flat method and weave in ends. ∎

Woven-top Hat

Use the loom to weave the top, then knit the sides, of this creative hat.

Skill Level

INTERMEDIATE

Sizes

Youth, adult
Instructions are given for smaller size, with larger size in parentheses. When only one number is given, it applies to both sizes.

Finished Measurements

Crown: 8 inches (10 inches) across
Sides: 3½ inches high

Materials

- Lion Brand Wool-Ease Thick and Quick super bulky weight yarn (6 oz/106 yd/170g per skein): 1 skein grass #131
- Green (Yellow) Knifty Knitter round loom [36 (41) pegs]
- Tapestry needle
- Crochet hook
- Hook tool

Gauge

4 inches = 9 stitches, 15 rows in twisted stockinette (e-wrap) stitch
Gauge does not need to be exact.

Instructions

Cut two pieces of yarn 20 feet (26 feet) long each.

Weave top of hat, using the two stands of yarn as one, taking care to not twist the yarn strands. (See Weaving Instructions)

Row 1: Starting at peg 1, with a single strand of yarn, knit (e-wrap) around the entire loom.

Row 2: Purl around the entire loom.

Rows 3–10: Knit. (e-wrap)

Row 11: Purl.

Row 12: Knit. (e-wrap)

Row 13: Purl.

Row 14: Knit. (e-wrap)

Bind off using the flat method, and weave in ends.

Weaving Instructions

Make a slip knot and put it on the anchor peg.

Bring yarn across to the opposite side of the loom at peg(s) 18 & 19 (21).

Loop around the outside of peg(s) from right to left, and bring the yarn back to the first side of the loom. Always make sure the yarn strands don't twist around each other.

Loop the yarn around the outside of pegs 1 and 36 (41).

Bring the yarn back to the opposite side of the loom around peg 20 (22).

"Kink" working yarn by folding. Bring the kinked loop of the yarn under the first double strand of yarn and over the second double strand of yarn to peg 17 (20), and hook on peg.

Pull kinked loop down to peg 2 and hook on peg. Bring working yarn around peg 35 (40). The yarn traveling between pegs 2 and 35 (40) stays on the inside of the loom.

Bring the yarn up to peg 21 (23).

"Kink" the yarn and pull the kinked loop of yarn under, over, under, and over the already strung yarn. Hook it on peg 16 (19).

Pull "kink" down and hook it on peg 3. The yarn will already be woven on the anchor peg side of the loom.

Hook the yarn on peg 34 (39), then peg 22 (24).

Continue until all pegs have been wrapped, making sure to keep yarn to the inside of the pegs. Always weave the loop of yarn under the first double strand. The weaving will look very loose, especially in the center.

Green loom only: To weave the last row, bring yarn to the outside of pegs 9 and 10. Wrap to the outside of peg 28. Weave back to opposite side, leaving working yarn to hang on the outside of loom between pegs 9–10.

Yellow loom only: To weave the last row, take the working yarn between pegs 32 and 31, wrap to the outside of peg 31 (peg 32 is empty). Weave the cut end through to the opposite side of the loom, e-wrap peg 11 with the working cut yarn to knit off on next row. ∎

Popcorn Bobble Hat

Popcorn bobbles decorate a hat that is as fun to knit as it is to wear.

Skill Level

EASY

Sizes

Youth, adult
Instructions are given for smaller size, with larger size in parentheses. When only one number is given, it applies to both sizes.

Finished Measurements

18 inches diameter, 7½ inches (8½ inches) brim to crown

Materials

- Lion Brand Wool Ease Thick and Quick super bulky weight yarn (6 oz/106 yd/170g per skein): 1 skein Fisherman #099
- Green Knifty Knitter round loom (36 pegs)
- Hook tool
- Tapestry needle
- Crochet hook

Gauge

4 inches = 9 stitches, 12 rows
Gauge does not need to be exact.

Pattern Note

All knit stitches are e-wrap (twisted stockinette).

Popcorn Bobble Stitch

This stitch is made by wrapping and knitting off the same peg several times, then catching the inside of the first stitch to tighten the bobble.

Step 1: Knit to the point where bobble is to be made.

Step 2: E-wrap the peg and knit off. Repeat 3 times on same peg.

Step 3: E-wrap the next peg and knit off.

Step 4: On the inside of the loom, the yarn strands coming from the pegs on either side of the bobble peg make a "v" pointing to the first stitch of the bobble. (Photo 1) Put the hook tool into the loop of the first bobble stitch; then bring this loop onto the bobble peg and knit off.

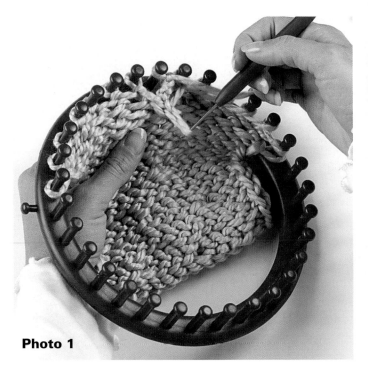

Photo 1

Instructions

Crochet cast on to pegs 1–36. Knit off peg 1, bringing the bottom loop over the top loop.

Row 1: Knit peg 1, purl peg 2, continue knitting the odd numbered pegs and purling the even numbered pegs to the end of the row.

Rows 2–4: Rep row 1.

Row 5: Knit.

Row 6: *Knit pegs 1–4. [Wrap peg 4 again and knit off] 3 times. On the inside of the loom, bring up the first loop of the four stitches and put it back on the peg. (See Photo 1.) Knit this loop: rep from* to end of row.

Row 7: Knit.

Row 8: Knit pegs 1–2. [Wrap peg 2 again and knit off] 3 times. On the inside of the loom, bring up the first loop of the four stitches and put it back on the peg. Knit off. *Knit 4, [wrap peg 6 again and knit off] 3 times. On the inside of the loom, bring up the first loop of the four stitches and put it back on the peg. Knit this loop: rep from * to end of row.

Rows 9–20 (24): [Rep rows 5–8] 3 (4) times.

Row 21 (25): Knit.

Row 22 (26): Move the loop on peg 1 to peg 2, the loop on peg 3 to peg 4, continue around the loom, moving loops on odd numbered pegs to the adjacent even numbered pegs. E-wrap the pegs with two loops on them, passing the yarn behind the empty pegs (on the inside of the loom). Knit off all pegs with three loops, bringing the bottom two loops over the top loop.

Bind off with the gathered method and weave in ends. ■

Drawstring Purse

Eyelets and I-cord create a handy drawstring for this pretty purse.

Skill Level

INTERMEDIATE

Finished Measurements

8 x 9 x 6 inches

Materials

- Moda Dea Caché bulky weight yarn
  (1¾ oz/72 yd/50g per skein): 2 skeins
  Tootsie #2329
- Green Knifty Knitter round loom (36 pegs)
- Hook tool
- Tapestry needle
- Crochet hook
- Plastic canvas mesh (for purse bottom): 6¼ x 4⅝ inches oval

Gauge

4 inches = 8 stitches, 12 rows
Gauge does not need to be exact.

Pattern Notes

Hold 2 strands of yarn together as one.
Knit stitches are e-wrap (twisted stockinette).
The alternating knit and purl stitches create a ribbed pattern.

Instructions

Leaving an 18-inch tail, e-wrap cast on pegs 7–18.

Rows 1–8: Slip 1, knit to end of row. (This flap is half of the purse bottom.) Cut yarn, leaving an 18-inch tail.

Leaving an 18-inch tail, e-wrap cast on pegs 25–36, and rep rows 1–8 to make second half of purse bottom.

Row 9: E-wrap the entire loom and knit off the pegs that have two loops on them.

Row 10: Purl.

Rows 11–30: Knit.

Row 31–33: K1, P1 to end of row.

Note: *To create the ribbing in this pattern, in each subsequent row, knit stitches should be on top of knit stitches; and purl stitches should be on top of purl stitches.*

Row 34: Move loop on peg 7 to peg 8, loop on peg 17

to peg 18, loop on peg 25 to 26 and loop on peg 35 to peg 36. (Moving these loops will create the eyelets.) Knit the knit stitches and purl the purl stitches, e-wrapping the empty pegs.

Row 35: Rep row 31.

Bind off using the flat method. After pulling the cut end of the yarn through the loop, don't pull it snug against the knit fabric. Instead, thread the yarn onto a tapestry needle, run it under the first chain of the bind off, then bring it back through the top of the last loop to complete the bind-off chain pattern. Weave in ends.

Assembly

On the inside of the purse, using one of the yarn tails, sew the long cast-on edges together. Sew the short edges along the purl stitch edge to complete the flat bottom. Weave in ends. Place plastic canvas in bottom of purse to strengthen bottom.

Make an I-cord 36 inches long. (See I-cord, page 7). Do not remove from loom. Cut yarn, leaving a 6-inch tail, and thread tail onto the tapestry needle.

Thread the I-cord through the eyelets so the cord is inside the bag along the long sides, and outside the bag along the short sides. Remove the I-cord from the loom, and wrap the two live stitches around the beginning end of the I-cord. With the tapestry needle, secure the end stitches, matching the stitch pattern at the beginning of the I-cord. Hide both I-cord tails in the center of the I-cord. ■

Seed Stitch Spa Set

The seed stitch creates wonderful texture, and is reversible.

Note

The seed stitch is made by alternating knit and purl stitches within every row, and from row to row. In each row, knit above the purl stitches, and purl above the knit stitches.

Skill Level

EASY

Finished Measurements

Washcloth: 10 inches square
Soap Sack: 3 x 5 1/2 inches

Materials

- Lily Sugar and Cream medium (worsted) weight yarn (2 oz/95 yds/56g per skein): 2 skeins butter cream ombre #00222
- Blue Knifty Knitter round loom (24 pegs)
- Hook tool
- Tapestry needle
- Crochet hook

Gauge

4 inches = 9 stitches, 16 rows
Gauge does not need to be exact.

Pattern Notes

All knit stitches are flat (stockinette) knit.
Hold two strands of yarn together as one throughout.

Instructions

Washcloth

Crochet cast on 24 pegs.

Row 1: Slip 1, [K1, P1] to end of row.

[Rep row 1] until piece measures 10 inches.

Bind off using the flat method and weave in ends.

Soap Sack

Using the e-wrap cast-on method, cast on 12 pegs, using every other peg of the 24-peg loom.

Row 1: Knit in the round. [K1, P1] to end of row. (Pass the yarn behind the even numbered pegs which are not in use.)

Row 2: [P1, K1], to end of row. (Continue to pass the yarn behind the even numbered pegs which are not in use.)

Rows 3–16: [Rep rows 1 & 2] 7 times.

Row 17: Move the loop on peg 1 to peg 3, move the loop on peg 5 to peg 7, the loop on peg 9 to peg 11, the loop on peg 13 to 15, the loop on peg 17 to 19, and the loop on peg 21 to 23. [(Moving these loops will create the eyelets.) There are now 6 pegs with 2 loops on them, and sets of 3 empty pegs between each double looped peg.] Pass the yarn behind the first empty peg, then in front of the second empty peg, and behind the third empty peg in each set of three. E-wrap the pegs with two loops on them; then knit these pegs (now with three loops on them,) bringing up the two bottom loops over the top loop.

Row 18–19: Repeat rows 1–2.

Bind off using the flat method, and weave in ends.

Sew bottom closed along cast on edge.

Drawstring

Make an I-cord 16 inches long. (See I cord, page 7) Do not remove from loom. Cut yarn, leaving a 12-inch tail and thread tail onto the tapestry needle.

Weave the starting end of the I-cord through the eyelets at the top of the soap sack. Remove the I-cord from the loom, being careful not to drop the two live stitches. Wrap the two stitches around the beginning end of the I-cord. With the tapestry needle, secure the ending stitches, matching the stitch pattern at the beginning of the I-cord. Hide both I-cord tails in the center of the I-cord. ∎

Mobius Shawl

The checkerboard pattern, with two right sides, is perfect for the mobius twist.

Skill Level

INTERMEDIATE

Sizes

Medium, Large/Extra-Large, XXL
Instructions are given for smaller size, with larger sizes in parentheses. When only one number is given, it applies to all sizes.

Finished Measurements

15 x 45 (55, 65) inches

Materials

- Lion Brand Moonlight Mohair bulky weight yarn (1¾ oz/82 yds/50g per skein): 4 skeins Safari #203
- Yellow Knifty Knitter round loom (41 pegs)
- Hook Tool
- Tapestry needle
- Crochet hook

Gauge

4 inches = 9 stitches, 12 rows

Pattern Note

All knit stitches are flat (stockinette) knit.
This combination of knit and pearl stitches creates a wonderful checkerboard pattern.

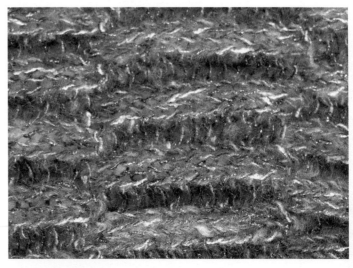

Instructions

E-wrap cast on 34 pegs.

Row 1: Slip 1, P1, [K2, P2] 7 times; K2, P1, K1.

Rows 2–15: Rep row 1.

Row 16: Slip 1, K1, [P2, K2] 8 times.

Rows 17–30: Rep row 16.

[Rep rows 1–30] 3 (4, 5) times.

[Rep rows 1–15] once.

Twisting the fabric once to create the mobius twist, put cast-on loops back onto the pegs.

Note: *When putting cast on edge back on loom, make sure that mobius strip does not trap the loom on the inside.*

Knit off, bringing bottom loop over top loop.

Remove from the loom with the flat bind-off method.

Weave in ends. ■

Diamond Lace Shawl

This elegant diamond-lace-stitch shawl will dress up your wardrobe.

Skill Level

EXPERIENCED

Finished Measurements

19 x 60 inches

Materials

- Moda Dea Dream medium (worsted) weight yarn (1¾ oz/93 yds/50g): 4 skeins Plum #3503
- Yellow Knifty Knitter round loom (41 pegs)
- Hook tool
- Tapestry needle
- Crochet hook
- Stitch markers

4 MEDIUM

Gauge

4 inches = 8 stitches in pattern, 10 rows.
Gauge does not need to be exact.

Pattern Notes

All knit stitches are e-wrap (twisted stockinette) stitches. Place stitch markers on pegs 2, 3, 4, 38, 39 and 40 before casting on, as a reminder that these pegs are purled on even numbered rows.

Start new skeins at the beginning of a row.

Diamond Lace Stitch Pattern

The lace pattern is worked in sets of two pegs.

Step 1: Bring the working yarn behind the first peg (on the inside of the loom).

Step 2: Wrap the yarn in front of and around the second peg clockwise so it comes to the outside of the loom between the two pegs.

Step 3: Bring the yarn in front of and around the first peg, counterclockwise to inside of loom.

The yarn is now in a figure-8.

Step 4: Knit off both pegs.

Step 5: Bring the yarn behind the second peg and continue with the third and fourth pegs.

Step 6: Continue in this manner with each subsequent pair of pegs.

Instructions

Crochet cast on 41 pegs.

Row 1: Slip 1, knit to end of row.

Row 2: Slip 1, purl to last peg, knit last peg.

Row 3: Rep row 1.

Row 4: Rep row 2.

Row 5: Rep row 1.

Row 6: Slip 1, P3, [Diamond Lace Stitch Pattern] 16 times, K1, P3, K1.

Row 7: Rep row 1.

Row 8: Slip 1, P3, K1, [Diamond Lace Stitch Pattern] 16 times, P3, K1.

[Rep rows 5–8] until shawl is 59 inches long.

Rep rows 1–5.

Bind off using the flat method and weave in ends. ∎

Shell Stitch Afghan

The shell stitch provides beautiful detail in this warm afghan.

Skill Level

EXPERIENCED

Finished Measurements

57 x 60 inches

Materials

- Red Heart Fiesta (6 oz/316 yds/170g per skein): 11 skeins Baby White #6301
- Yellow Knifty Knitter round loom (41 pegs)
- Hook tool
- Tapestry needle
- Crochet hook
- Stitch markers

MEDIUM

Gauge

4 inches = 11 stitches, 16 rows
Gauge does not need to be exact.

Pattern Notes

All knit stitches are flat knit (stockinette) stitch.
The instructions for left and right sides assume peg 2 is to the left of peg 1.
The shell stitch uses 5 pegs, with two knit pegs to either side between the "shells," and 3 rows of flat (stockinette) knitting between the shell rows.
Note: *When knitting the shell stitch, make sure the stitches are loose enough to move easily from one peg to another.*

Instructions
Center (make two)

Note: *Put stitch markers of one color on pegs 2, 8, 9, 15, 16, 22, 23, 29, 30 36, and 37 to remind you which pegs always get knit on the shell stitch pattern rows. Put stitch markers of another color on pegs 5, 12, 19, 26 and 33 to mark the pegs in the center of the shell; these will be knit off as a one-under-three purl stitch on the shell stitch pattern rows.*

Crochet cast on 37 pegs.

Row 1: Sl 1, P35, K1.

Row 2: Sl 1, K36.

Row 3: Sl 1, P35, K1.

Rows 4–8: Sl 1, K36.

Row 9 (Shell Stitch Row): Sl 1, K1, [Move the loop on peg 4 to peg 5, the loop on peg 3 to peg 4, the loop on peg 6 to peg 5, and the loop on peg 7 to peg 6. Pass the working yarn in front of empty peg 3, purl peg 4, purl peg 5, bringing the new loop through all three existing loops on the peg at once; purl peg 6, pass the working yarn in front of empty peg 7, K2] 5 times.

(Photo 1 shows how the loops are set up before being knit off.)

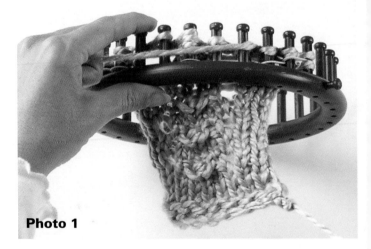

Photo 1

[Rep rows 6–9] until piece measures 57 inches.
[Rep rows 4–8] once.
[Rep rows 1–3] once.
Bind off using the flat method, and weave in ends.

Right side

Note: *Put stitch markers of one color on pegs 6, 7, 13, 14, 20, 21, 27, 28, 34, and 35 to remind you which pegs always get knit on the shell stitch pattern rows. Put stitch markers of another color on pegs 10, 17, 24 and 31 to mark the pegs in the center of the shell; these will be knit off as a one-under-three purl stitch on the shell stitch pattern rows. Put stitch markers of a third color on pegs 2–5 to remind you to purl these pegs on odd numbered rows.*

Crochet cast on 35 pegs.

Row 1: Sl 1, P33, K1.

Row 2: Sl 1, K34.

Row 3: Rep row 1.

Row 4: Rep row 2.

Row 5: Sl 1, P4, K30.

Row 6: Rep row 2.

Row 7: Rep row 5.

Row 8: Rep row 2.

Row 9 (Shell Stitch Row): Sl 1, P4, K2, [move the loop on peg 9 to peg 10, the loop on peg 8 to peg 9, the loop on peg 11 to peg 10, and the loop on peg 12 to peg 11. Pass the yarn in front of empty peg 8, purl pegs 9–11, pass the yarn in front of empty peg 12, K2] 4 times.

[Rep rows 6–9] until piece measures 57 inches.

[Rep rows 4–8] once.

[Rep rows 1–3] once.

Bind off using the flat method and weave in ends.

Left side

Note: *Put stitch markers of one color on pegs 2, 8, 9, 15, 16, 22, 23, 29 and 30 to remind you which pegs always get knit on the pattern rows. Put stitch markers of another color on pegs 5, 12, 19 and 26 to mark the pegs in the center of the shell; these will be knit off as a one-under-three purl stitch on the pattern rows. Put stitch markers of a third color on pegs 31–34 to remind you to purl these pegs on odd numbered rows.*

Crochet cast on 35 pegs

Row 1: Sl 1, P33, K1.

Row 2: Sl 1, K34.

Row 3: Rep row 1.

Row 4: Rep row 2.

Row 5: Sl 1, K30, P3, K1.

Row 6: Rep row 2.

Row 7: Rep row 5.

Row 8: Rep row 2.

Row 9 (Shell Stitch Row): Sl 1, K1, [move the loop on peg 4 to peg 5, the loop on peg 3 to peg 4, the loop on peg 6 to peg 5, and the loop on peg 7 to peg 6. Pass the yarn in front of empty peg 3, purl pegs 4–6, pass the yarn in front of empty peg 7, K2] 4 times, P4, K1.

[Rep rows 6–9] until piece measures 57 inches.

[Rep rows 4–8] once.

[Rep rows 1–3] once.

Bind off using the flat method, and weave in ends.

Assembly

Block pieces. Sew panels together using one strand of yarn and weave in all ends. ∎

Chevron Baby Blanket

This chevron stitch pattern is easy to create using a combination of knit and purl stitches.

Skill Level

EXPERIENCED

Finished Measurements

37 x 35 inches

Materials

- Red Heart Soft Baby lightweight yarn (7 oz/575 yds/198g per skein): 3 skeins Lilac #7588

MEDIUM

- Red Heart Baby Econo medium (worsted) weight yarn (6 oz/460 yds/170g per skein): 3 skeins Lavender #1570
- Blue Knifty Knitter round loom (24 pegs)
- Blue Knifty Knitter oval loom (62 pegs)
- Hook tool
- Tapestry needle
- Crochet hook
- Stitch markers

Gauge

4 inches in pattern = 11 stitches, 20 rows
Gauge does not need to be exact.

Pattern Notes

All knit stitches are e-wrap (twisted stockinette) stitches. Hold one strand of each yarn together, treating the two strands as one throughout.

Before casting on, put stitch markers of one color on every eighth peg starting with peg 2, and markers of a second color on every eighth peg starting with peg 6, to show the top and bottom points of each chevron. There will be an equal number of knit or purl stitches on either side of each marker.

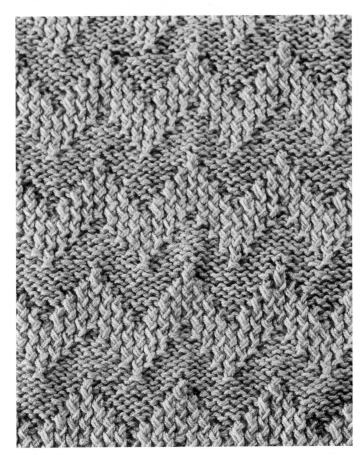

Instructions

Center panel

Crochet cast on 59 pegs.

Rows 1 & 2: Sl 1, [P1, K7] 7 times, P1, K1.

Rows 3 & 4: Sl 1, P2, [K5, P3] 6 times, K5, P2, K1.

Rows 5 & 6: Sl 1, P3, [K3, P5] 6 times, K3, P3, K1.

Rows 7 & 8: Sl 1, P4, [K1, P7] 6 times, K1, P4, K1.

Rows 9 & 10: Sl 1, [K1, P7] 7 times, K2.

Rows 11 & 12: Sl 1, K2, [P5, K3] 6 times, P5, K3.

Rows 13 & 14: Sl 1, K3, [P3, K5] 6 times, P3, K4.

Rows 15 & 16: Sl 1, K4, [P1, K7] 6 times, P1, K5.

[Rep rows 1–16] until piece measures 35 inches.

Bind off using the flat method and weave in ends.

Side panels (make two)

Crochet cast on 19 pegs.

Row 1: Sl 1, K4, P1, K7, P1, K5.

Row 2: Sl 1, P5, K7, P5, K1.

Row 3: Sl 1, K4, P2, K5, P2, K5.

Row 4: Sl 1, P6, K5, P6, K1.

Row 5: Sl 1, K4, P3, K3, P3, K5.

Row 6: Sl 1, P7, K3, P7, K1.

Row 7: Sl 1, K4, P4, K1, P4, K5.

Row 8: Sl 1, P8, K1, P8, K1.

Row 9: Sl 1, K5, P7, K6.

Row 10: Sl 1, P4, K1, P7, K1, P4, K1.

Row 11: Sl 1, K6, P5, K7.

Row 12: Sl 1, P4, K2, P5, K2, P4, K1.

Row 13: Sl 1, K7, P3, K8.

Row 14: Sl 1, P4, K3, P3, K3, P4, K1.

Row 15: Sl 1, K8, P1, K9.

Row 16: Sl 1, P4, K4, P1, K4, P4, K1.

[Rep rows 1–16] until piece measures 35 inches.

Bind off using the flat method and weave in ends.

Assembly

Match the chevron pattern on the side panels to the chevron pattern on the center panel. Join seams, catching the slipped stitches from both panels. Weave in all ends. ■

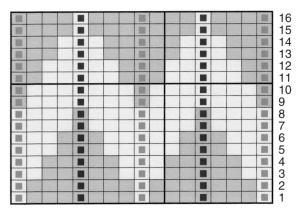

CENTER PANEL CHART

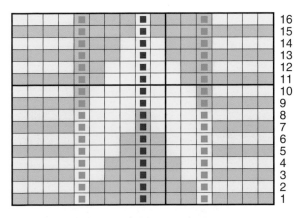

SIDE PANEL CHART

STITCH KEY
- Knit
- Purl
- First color marker
- Second color marker

Abbreviations & Symbols

approx .... approximately
beg .... begin/beginning
CC .... contrasting color
cm .... centimeter(s)
dec .... decrease/decreases/decreasing
g .... gram
inc .... increase/increases/increasing
k .... knit
LH .... left hand
lp(s) .... loop(s)
m .... meter(s)
MC .... main color
mm .... millimeter(s)
oz .... ounce(s)
p .... purl
pat(s) .... pattern(s)
rem .... remain/remaining

rep .... repeat(s)
RH .... right hand
rnd(s) .... rounds
RS .... right side
sl .... slip
st(s) .... stitch(es)
St st .... stockinette stitch/stocking stitch
tog .... together
WS .... wrong side
yd(s) .... yard(s)

[ ] work instructions within brackets as many times as directed

( ) work instructions within parentheses in the place directed

** repeat instructions following the asterisks as directed

* repeat instructions following the single asterisk as directed

" inch(es)

Standard Yarn Weight System

Categories of yarn, gauge ranges, and recommended needle sizes

Yarn Weight Symbol & Category Names	1 SUPER FINE	2 FINE	3 LIGHT	4 MEDIUM	5 BULKY	6 SUPER BULKY
Type of Yarns in Category	Sock, Fingering, Baby	Sport, Baby	DK, Light Worsted	Worsted, Afghan, Aran	Chunky, Craft, Rug	Bulky, Roving
Knit Gauge Range* in Stockinette Stitch to 4 inches	27–32 sts	23–26 sts	21–24 sts	16–20 sts	12–15 sts	6–11 sts
Recommended Needle in Metric Size Range	2.25–3.25mm	3.25–3.75mm	3.75–4.5mm	4.5–5.5mm	5.5–8mm	8mm and larger
Recommended Needle U.S. Size Range	1 to 3	3 to 5	5 to 7	7 to 9	9 to 11	11 and larger

* GUIDELINES ONLY: The above reflect the most commonly used gauges and needle sizes for specific yarn categories.

Metric Charts

INCHES INTO MILLIMETERS & CENTIMETERS (Rounded off slightly)

inches	mm	cm	inches	cm	inches	cm	inches	cm
1/8	3	0.3	5	12.5	21	53.5	38	96.5
1/4	6	0.6	5 1/2	14	22	56	39	99
3/8	10	1	6	15	23	58.5	40	101.5
1/2	13	1.3	7	18	24	61	41	104
5/8	15	1.5	8	20.5	25	63.5	42	106.5
3/4	20	2	9	23	26	66	43	109
7/8	22	2.2	10	25.5	27	68.5	44	112
1	25	2.5	11	28	28	71	45	114.5
1 1/4	32	3.2	12	30.5	29	73.5	46	117
1 1/2	38	3.8	13	33	30	76	47	119.5
1 3/4	45	4.5	14	35.5	31	79	48	122
2	50	5	15	38	32	81.5	49	124.5
2 1/2	65	6.5	16	40.5	33	84	50	127
3	75	7.5	17	43	34	86.5		
3 1/2	90	9	18	46	35	89		
4	100	10	19	48.5	36	91.5		
4 1/2	115	11.5	20	51	37	94		

Skill Levels

BEGINNER
Beginner projects for first-time knitters using basic stitches. Minimal shaping.

EASY
Easy projects using basic stitches, repetitive stitch patterns, simple color changes and simple shaping and finishing.

INTERMEDIATE
Intermediate projects with a variety of stitches, mid-level shaping and finishing.

EXPERIENCED
Experienced projects using advanced techniques and stitches, detailed shaping and refined finishing.

We wish to thank ProvoCraft for generously providing all of the
Knifty Knitter™ Looms used in the instructional photographs.

DRG Publishing
306 East Parr Road
Berne, IN 46711

ISBN: 978-1-59012-192-4